ABUNDANT TRUTH INTERNATIONAL MINISTRIES

Biblical Studies Series

The Covenants Speak

An Examination of the Adamic and of the Noahic Covenants

Roderick Levi Evans

The Covenants Speak

An Examination of the Adamic and of the Noahic Covenants

All Rights Reserved ©2009 by Roderick L. Evans

Front & Back Cover Designs by Abundant Truth Publishing All Rights Reserved.
Image by Welcome to All ! ツ from Pixabay

Abundant Truth Publishing
an imprint of Abundant Truth International Ministries

For information address:
Abundant Truth International
P.O. Box 126
Camden, NC 27921

Unless otherwise indicated, all of the scripture quotations are taken from the *Authorized King James Version* **of the Bible. Scripture quotations marked with NIV are taken from the** *New International Version* **of the Bible. Scripture quotations marked with ASV are taken from the** *American Standard Version* **of the Bible. Scripture quotations marked with GW are taken from the** *God's Word Bible***.**

ISBN 13: 978-1-60141-505-9

Printed in the United States of America.

Contents

Preface

Introduction

STUDY 1 – The Adamic Covenant 1

Lesson 1 - And God Said	**3**
The Citation of the Covenant	8
The Prelude to the Covenant	28
The Institution of the Covenant	30
Lesson 2 - And the Lord God Commanded	**37**
The Covenant Humbles Man	39
The Covenant Challenges Man	42
The Character of the Covenant	46
Lesson 3 - Of Every Tree thou Mayest Eat	**53**
The Command of the Covenant	55
The Consequence of the Covenant	57

Contents (cont.)

The Conclusion of the Covenant   62

STUDY 2 – The Noahic Covenant   67

Lesson 1 - And It Repented the Lord   69
The Presentation of the Covenant   75
The Prelude to the Covenant   77
The Institution of the Covenant   87

Lesson 2 - For in these Things I Delight   91
Holiness Causes the Covenant   95
Righteousness Causes the Covenant   97
Love Causes the Covenant   98

Lesson 3 - But Noah found Grace   103
Noah's Example before the Covenant   105

Contents (cont.)

Noah's Example after the Covenant   113

Lesson 4 - This is the Token of the Covenant...   121

The Promises of the Covenant   123

The Sign of the Covenant   136

Lesson 5 – The Covenant and the Faith   143

Noah's Example Reflects the Christian Faith   146

Noah's Experience Reflects the End Times and Judgment   148

Bibliography   153

Preface

What is a covenant? A biblical covenant is an agreement between God and man that governs their relationship. In the scriptures, a covenant was more than an impersonal contract, but a symbol of God's faithfulness and man's responsibility in worship.

In both testaments, God established covenants with man. It is my hope to bring clarity to two biblical covenants. It is my prayer that as each covenant is explored, the reader will develop a clearer understanding of God's eternal purpose and power.

Roderick Levi Evans

Introduction

Paul instructed Timothy to rightly divide the Word of Truth. In order to do this as believers we should follow this example and become students of the Bible. The Biblical Studies Series was developed to aid believers in the study of the various scriptures and foundational doctrines.

In this publication:

In this study, we will explore two foundational covenants of God's interaction with His creation. We will examine the Adamic and the Noahic Covenants. First, we will explore the Adamic Covenant; that is, the first man's relationship with God.

Though the terms of man's interaction with God was not defined by the word *covenant,* it is implied that God established a covenant with him.

God's relationship with the first man provides insight into the requirements placed upon the Christian today. Christians can learn from Adam's conformity and contravention of God's command to him. To understand God's plan and eternal purpose for believers today, Adam's relationship serves as an example.

After exploring the Adamic Covenant, we will, secondly, explore the Noahic Covenant. God established this covenant after destroying the earth with the Flood. It was the first time in biblical history that the word covenant is introduced.

The Noahic Covenant differed from those that would follow because it involved all of creation as well man and his descendants. This covenant reveals God's ultimate plan of judgment and salvation. As we explore these two Covenants, we will see God's eternal purpose for the Christian today.

The Covenants Speak

-STUDY 1-
THE ADAMIC COVENANT

God's Covenant with the First Man

Biblical Studies Series

The Covenants Speak

The Covenants Speak

-Lesson 1-
And God Said

The Covenants Speak

The first book of the Hebrew and Christian scriptures is *Genesis*. It comes from a word that means "beginning." Genesis functions as the introduction to the rest of the scriptures.

Have ye not known? Have ye not heard? Hath it not been told you from the beginning? Have ye not understood from the foundations of the earth? (Isaiah 40:21)

Understanding the accounts of Genesis is important to comprehending the totality of the work of God in the earth. The scriptures tell us that God declares the end from the beginning. Genesis reveals to us God's eternal purpose for man to live with Him forever in heaven as the first man who walked with Him in the garden.

> *And the Lord God planted a garden eastward in Eden; and there he put the man whom he had formed. (Genesis 2:8)*

The Book of Genesis answers all questions concerning the origin of the universe. From within its pages, we discover the origin of mankind, the origin of the planets and stars, the origin of all life forms, and the origin of sin and evil. It is also provides the basis for God's ultimate plan of redemption for the man that He created.

> *And I will put enmity between thee and the woman, and between thy seed and her seed; it shall bruise thy head, and thou shalt bruise his heel. (Genesis 3:15)*

Moreover, it is also within the account of the origin of the first man that we see the origins of man's relationship with God. Within this relationship, we discover the implications of the first covenant.

The Citation of the Covenant

Before the creation of the man with whom He would establish relationship and covenant, God patiently brought the world into a livable habitation. Let us now review the order of God's creation and its application to God's eternal purpose.

I.   **The First Day – Light.** The earth was covered with darkness. In order to the darkness, God spoke light into existence and gave it definition. He called it Day. The darkness, He called Night.

And God said, Let there be light:

and there was light. And God saw the light, that it was good: and God divided the light from the darkness. And God called the light Day, and the darkness he called Night. And the evening and the morning were the first day. (Genesis 1:3-5)

Application – These verses teach us that the absence of God darkness. God did not actively create darkness. It existed where He was not active. However, He did speak light into existence. By giving light and darkness the names of Day and Night respectively, God gives a sign in creation of righteousness versus unrighteousness.

God shows a heavenly distinction of clean and unclean; holy and unholy; children of light (God) and children of darkness (devil). Even as the light invaded the darkness, the glorious light of the gospel invades the darkness of the soul bound by sin.

II. The Second Day – Sky and Atmosphere. God divides the waters upon the earth downward and upward. The waters came together above to form the heavens.

And God said, Let there be a firmament in the midst of the waters, and let it divide the waters from the waters. And God made the firmament, and divided the waters which were under the firmament from the waters which were above the firmament: and it was so. And God called the firmament Heaven. And the evening and the morning were the second day. (Genesis 1:6-8)

Application – These verses teach us that God is above. He called the skies heaven, the same term used to describe His dwelling. Just as the rains would eventually come down from the skies to give water to the earth, man was to look up to heaven for God's blessing, strength, and direction.

III. The Third Day – The Earth, Seas, and Grass.

Next, God caused the waters that were below the heavens to gather so dry land would appear. After the land appeared, it was clothed with grass, herbs, and all manner of plant life.

> *And God said, Let the waters under the Heaven be gathered together*

unto one place, and let the dry land appear: and it was so. And God called the dry land Earth; and the gathering together of the waters called the Seas: and God saw that it was good. And God said, Let the earth bring forth grass, the herb yielding seed, and the fruit tree yielding fruit after his kind, whose seed is in itself, upon the earth: and it was so. And the earth brought forth grass, and herb yielding seed after his kind, and the tree yielding fruit, whose seed was in itself, after his kind: and God saw that it was good. And the evening and the morning were the third day.

Application – God separated the waters covering the land to cause dry land to appear and vegetation to grow. When one is converted, he no longer is lost in the seas of sin. He is able to come up as dry land and produce fruit in righteousness.

Sin no longer dominates and is kept back by the boundaries of man's obedience. Sin may come up to tempt man as the waves come up to the coasts, but it has no control over him as he walks with Christ.

IV. **The Fourth Day – Sun, Moon, & Stars put in place.** After the land came forward, God placed the sun, moon, and stars in place. One great light (the Sun) was to rule the day, while the lesser (the Moon) would rule the night. The stars would also take part in giving light.

> *And God said, Let there be lights in the firmament of the heaven to divide the day from the night; and let them be for signs, and for seasons, and for days, and years: And let them*

be for lights in the firmament of the heaven to give light upon the earth: and it was so. And God made two great lights; the greater light to rule the day, and the lesser light to rule the night: he made the stars also. And God set them in the firmament of the heaven to give light upon the earth, And to rule over the day and over the night, and to divide the light from the darkness: and God saw that it was good. And the evening and the morning were the fourth day. (Genesis 1:14-19)

Application – The Sun, Moon, and stars were given to light the world. Since now, the world is in spiritual darkness, the Sun, Moon, and stars represent Jesus, the believers, and the angels respectively. Lights were given to overcome darkness. God sent Jesus as the light of the world. He needed no assistance. As the Sun rules in the day, while Christ was in the earth, He was the Light of the world.

Science teaches that in order for the moon and stars to shine, they need the light of the Sun. After Jesus' resurrection, His followers became the lights of the world. They were to shine in darkness as the moon does at night. The believers need the light of Jesus to shine through them to a dark and dying world (as the moon needs the Sun's light).

In scriptures, the term 'stars' is used to describe angels. God promised that His angels would protect and minister to believers.

In addition, the angels were used at times to bring God's message to man. Thus, as stars supplement the moon's light so do angels aid the servants of God and Jesus in this world.

V. **The Fifth Day – Marine Life and Winged Flying Birds.** God expands life on the earth to life in the sea and the skies. The waters were populated with numerous types of marine species. The winged birds were seen flying in the air abundantly.

And God said, Let the waters bring forth abundantly the moving creature that hath life, and fowl that may fly above the earth in the open firmament of heaven. And God created great whales, and every living creature that moveth, which the waters brought forth abundantly, after their kind, and every winged fowl after his kind: and God saw that it was good. And God blessed them, saying, Be fruitful, and multiply, and fill the waters in the seas, and let fowl multiply in the earth. And the evening and the morning were the fifth day. (Genesis 1:20-23)

Application – God's expansion of creation shows the magnitude of the authority of the believer. God gave the man dominion over all His creation. Even the birds of the air are subject to man. In like manner, the believer has authority over all the works of the devil, who is called the prince of the power of the air.

In addition, the population of marine life reflects the believers as fishers of men. As man's diet would change from vegetation to flesh, the believer's walk turns fro walking in righteousness to bringing others into the righteousness that comes from belief in Christ.

VI. The Sixth Day – Man and All Living Creatures. To conclude His creation, God created all the beasts and living creatures of the earth. Then, He created man as the crown of His creation.

And God said, Let the earth bring forth the living creature after his kind, cattle, and creeping thing, and beast of the earth after his kind: and it was so. And God made the beast of the earth after his kind, and cattle after their kind, and everything that creepeth upon the earth after his kind: and God saw that it was good. And God said, Let us make man in our image, after our likeness: and let them have dominion over the fish of the sea, and over the fowl of the air, and over the cattle, and over all the earth, and over every creeping thing that creepeth upon the earth. And God saw every thing that he had made, and, behold, it was very good. And the evening and the morning were the sixth day. (Genesis 1:24-26, 31)

Application – God created both man and beast during the same time. This introduces some biblical truths. The first is that the relationship between believers and unbelievers is reflected. The male and female reflect those who have come into relationship with God through Jesus as a son or daughter.

The various beasts of the field represent unbelievers who are under Satan's control. They are not walking as children of God, but as animals who only live to eat and satisfy their desire to live.

The male and female reflect those who are striving to be like the Son of God, while the animals reflect the unbeliever's drive to survive. The male and female and the animals all came from the earth. This means their external experiences in life will be the same. This reflects how God sends rain on the just and the unjust.

Just as He provides for all creation, He will provide and sometimes bless those who do not serve Him. In addition, man and beast are seen together for they both will share in God's redemptive work in the earth. The scriptures declare that all of creation groans with the believers in expectation of Christ's coming.

Because the creature itself also shall be delivered from the bondage of corruption into the glorious liberty of the children of God. For we know that the whole creation groaneth and travaileth in pain together until now. (Romans 8:21-22)

VII. The Seventh Day – God Rests. On the seventh day, God saw His works as very good and He rested.

Thus the heavens and the earth were finished, and all the host of them. And on the seventh day God ended his work which he had made; and he rested on the seventh day from all his work which he had made. And God blessed the seventh day, and sanctified it: because that in it he had rested from all his work which God created and made. (Genesis 2:1-3)

Application – God's rest on the seventh day demonstrates to believers that there is a rest coming for them. As God completed His labors and rested, believers who endure to the end will enter into eternal rest with Him.

God's rest serves as an example to all creation that when they have labored, they will take time to enjoy the works of their hands. The writer of Ecclesiastes echoes this sentiment when he states that to labor and enjoy the fruit of it is the gift of God.

The Prelude to the Covenant

All of the events of creation occurred prior to the coming covenant with the man. After God created the man, He gave them a charge, which preceded the covenant.

> *So God created man in his own image, in the image of God created he him; male and female created he them. And God blessed them, and God said unto them, Be*

fruitful, and multiply, and replenish the earth, and subdue it: and have dominion over the fish of the sea, and over the fowl of the air, and over every living thing that moveth upon the earth. (Genesis 1:27-28)

God gave five exhortations to them. The first was to be fruitful. Next, they were to multiply. Then, they were to replenish (fill) the earth.

Finally, they were to exercise dominion over all of the living creatures. Continuing, they were to subdue the earth. Fina of sky and sea. Believers should follow these exhortations of the beginning today.

> *For whatsoever things were written aforetime were written for our learning, that we through patience and comfort of the scriptures might have hope. Romans 15:4 (KJV)*

On the following page, we have provided a table outlining the exhortations to the first man and their implication on the Christian today.

The Institution of the Covenant

After these things, God placed man in the garden that He planted. In addition, man was to take care of the garden.

> *And the Lord God planted a garden eastward in Eden; and there he put the man whom he had formed. And the Lord God took the man and put him into the garden of Eden to dress it and to keep it. (Genesis 2:8, 15)*

God wanted to establish relationship with man, thus God laid a foundation for this relationship.

> *And the Lord God commanded the man, saying, Of every tree of the garden thou mayest freely eat: But*

of the tree of the knowledge of good and evil, thou shalt not eat of it: for in the day that thou eatest thereof thou shalt surely die.(Genesis 2:16-17)

The foundation for the Adamic Covenant rested upon one command; man was not to eat from one of the trees in the garden.

On the following page, we have developed a diagram showing the parallels between the exhortations given to first man and those that are given to the New Testament believer. This illustrates how the plan of redemption was always in the mind of God.

The Exhortation to Man	*The Exhortation to the Believer*
Be Fruitful	The believer is to be fruitful in his or her relationship with Christ; that is, growing in grace and character. (Rmns. 6:22; 2 Ptr. 1:8)
Multiply	The believer is to spread the gospel and win others to Christ. (Matt. 4:19)
Replenish (Fill) the earth	The believer is to fill the earth with the knowledge of God, through Jesus. (Habakkuk 2:14)

Subdue the earth	The believer is to walk in victory over the world and its influences. (I John 5:4)
Have Dominion	The believer has power and authority over all the works of the devil. (Luke 10:19)

Notes:

-Lesson 2-
And the Lord God Commanded

God came into covenant with Adam. Adam had to refrain from one tree and the Adamic Covenant would be solidified. When one considers the account of creation, the most obvious question surfaces: "Why did God place the tree in the garden?" The response to this question helps us to understand the command of the Adamic Covenant.

The Covenant Humbles Man

Adam and Eve were created sinless. They did not know good and evil; they only knew God. This introduces us to an important truth. In the beginning, man was expected to know God; not good and evil.

When the knowledge of good and evil eventually comes, man refused to walk with God. Moreover, man became judges of what is right and wrong. Man became a law unto himself forgetting the God that created Him.

> *Because that, when they knew God, they glorified him not as God, neither were thankful; but became vain in their imaginations, and their foolish heart was darkened. Professing themselves to*

be wise, they became fools. (Romans 1:21-22)

God placed man over the works of His hands. Man only knew how to subdue and have dominion. Thus, God established His authority over man with the command. God instituted the command to remind man of his position before the Lord. Every time man saw the tree of the knowledge of good and evil, he remembered the command and who gave it.

The same principle applies to the believer. Though Christ is our brother and friend, He is equally our Lord. We become the children of God as He is. However, Jesus' role before God is greater than ours, for He is the only begotten son of the Father. We become children by faith, but He is the Son forever.

The Covenant Challenges Man

In this section, we find an answer to the proposed question of why God place that Tree in the garden. There are three discernable reasons why God planted the Tree of knowledge in the garden. The Tree of knowledge was placed in the garden because:

1. **God wanted to put it there.** He does not have to answer to anyone for His actions. In His wisdom, holiness, and righteous judgment, the Lord planted the Tree of knowledge with the others.

    Then answered the Lord unto Job out of the whirlwind, and said, Wilt thou also disannul my judgment? Wilt thou condemn me, that thou mayest be righteous? (Job 40:6, 8)

2. **God wanted to challenge man.** Man served God because he was created sinless. The placement of tree and man's

obedience to the command challenged man's service to be by choice; not by how he was created.

> *Hath not the potter power over the clay, of the same lump to make one vessel unto honour, and another unto dishonour? (Romans 9:21)*

3. **God wanted to teach us.** The placement of the Tree of knowledge in the garden demonstrates to the believer that the temptation to sin may always be there. When one is converted, the power of sin is broken. However, the believer has to resist partaking of the tree of the

knowledge of good and evil (sin) after Christ comes in.

When Christ came, sin did not leave the world, but He brought man back to the beginning. Mankind would now have a choice to sin or serve Him. The record of man's fall along with the Old Testament is designed to teach us and give us hope.

For whatsoever things were written aforetime were written for our learning, that we through patience and comfort of the scriptures might have hope. (Romans 15:4)

The Character of the Covenant

When God established the different covenants, He would choose an individual to receive and reveal the covenant to others. The main character of the Adamic Covenant, of course, is **Adam**. Genesis records that God gave the command of the covenant to him alone.

And the Lord God commanded the man... (Genesis 2:16a)

To complete His creation, God created man. Unlike all the other living creatures that were spoken into existence, God became personally involved in man's creation.

> *And the Lord God formed man of the dust of the ground, and breathed into his nostrils the beath of life; and man became a living soul. (Genesis 2:7)*

Man was not spoken into existence; he was formed. The word used for formed was **yatsar** *(pronounced yaw-tsar')*. It means to form through squeezing into shape, mould, form a pattern. Aside from the physical attributes of man, there were to be specific character traits that the man was to possess.

> *And God said, Let us make man in our image, after our likeness: and let them have dominion over the fish of the sea, and over the fowl of the air, and over the cattle, and over all the earth, and over every creeping thing that creepeth upon the earth. (Genesis 1:26)*

When God prepared to create man, He had two goals in mind. Man was to be created in His *image* and His *likeness*.

The word translated image is **tselem** *(it is pronounced tseh'-lem)*. It means representation or representative figure. This speaks of God's authority. Created in His image, **_Adam was to represent and operate in the authority of God._** This is reflected in the statement that man was to have dominion over all the earth.

The word translated _likeness_ is **_dmuth_** _(it is pronounced dem-ooth')_. It simply means resemblance. This speaks of God's character. Created in His likeness, **_Adam was to reflect and demonstrate the character and personality of God._** Man was to operate in the authority given to him as he reflected the nature of God.

Since Adam represented God's authority and reflected His character, the covenant that was instituted should not have been a point of stumbling to him.

Notes:

The Covenants Speak

-Lesson 3-
Of Every Tree Thou Mayest Eat

Since covenants are similar to contractual agreements, they have conditions and terms. The Adamic Covenant does not differ though it contains few elements. To understand God's intent for this covenant, an examination of its constitution is necessary. The Adamic Covenant contains two main components.

The Command of the Covenant

The first part of the covenant included permission to eat from every tree in the Garden. However, the command (and prohibition) came that only one tree could not be eaten from.

> *And the Lord God commanded the man, saying, Of every tree of the garden thou mayest freely eat: But of the tree of the knowledge of good and evil, thou shalt not eat of it. (Genesis 2:16-17a)*

The command was simple: Do not eat from only ONE tree in the garden. Man could eat from any of the other tress in the Garden. God told the man that he could **freely** eat of those trees also. He would be able to eat from them until his appetite was satiated.

Application – As believers, we have received the free gift of salvation. We are free from the law and its bondage. We are able to live this life free of fear, guilt, and shame.

Like Adam, only one prohibition is laid upon us. We are to abstain from sinful acts. A sinful act is an activity or attitude that is prohibited by the law of God (which includes His nature) expressly or implicitly. We are free to do many things, but only have one prohibition.

The Consequence of the Covenant

God outlines the terms of the

covenant with Adam precisely. If man ate of this tree, the result would be death.

> *But of the tree of the knowledge of good and evil, thou shalt not eat of it: for in the day that thou eatest thereof thou shalt surely die. (Genesis 2:17)*

God's words were exact. If the fruit of the Tree of knowledge was ingested, Adam would experience death. Since the complete story has unfolded, it may appear that God's warning did not happen. This is because Adam and Eve did not die immediately. However, it is impossible for God to lie.

> *That by two immutable things, in which it was impossible for God to lie, we might have a strong consolation, who have fled for refuge to lay hold upon the hope set before us. (Hebrews 6:18)*

There is a valid explanation. First, understand that God did not intend for man to live forever in his flesh. The inhabitants of the earth would only live for a period of time. If this was not so, God would not have prevented Adam and Eve from eating of the Tree of life that made one immortal.

> *And the Lord God said, Behold, the man is become as one of us, to know good and evil: and now, lest he put forth his hand, and take also of the tree of life, and eat, and live forever. (Genesis 3:22)*

Man would **die** (physically) regardless of the command. Without contradiction, the death that God spoke of had to be a *spiritual* death. The fruit that they ate would not affect their physical health, but their mental health. God knew the knowledge of good and evil would lead to the death of man's spiritual perception of God, and it would lead to the death of man's innocence before the Lord.

Application – This understanding of death coincides with the doctrine of Christ. While on earth, Christ stated that He came to give men life. Why would men need life if they were not physically dead?

Christ came to offer spiritual life; resulting in man's restoration to God. The believer has to guard against sin that produces death in the spiritual life.

The Conclusion of the Covenant

The Adamic Covenant never ended. Though the covenant was violated, God still commands man (especially those that have received Him) to abstain from sin. They are not to partake of things that are unholy, unclean, or unrighteous.

> *Be ye not unequally yoked together with unbelievers: for what fellowship hath righteousness with unrighteousness? and what communion hath light with darkness? And what concord hath Christ with Belial? or what part hath*

he that believeth with an infidel? And what agreement hath the temple of God with idols? for ye are the temple of the living God; as God hath said, I will dwell in them, and walk in them; and I will be their God, and they shall be my people. Wherefore come out from among them, and be ye separate, saith the Lord, and touch not the unclean thing; and I will receive you. And will be a Father unto you, and ye shall be my sons and daughters, saith the Lord

Almighty. (II Corinthians 6:1418)

Believers are instructed to shun the very appearance of evil. God sent Christ (called the last Adam) to restore man. The Adamic Covenant finds its fulfillment in Christ. He came and performed the first works of Adam. In addition, those that believe on Him are able to do so. The believer does this by adhering to the commands of the Lord in the scriptures.

Notes:

-STUDY 2-
THE NOAHIC COVENANT

"God's Covenant of Peace with all Creation"

-Lesson 1-
And It Repented the Lord

In the beginning, God created the heavens and the earth (Genesis 1:1). After the creation of land, sea, and the living creatures, the crown of God's creation was then formed. Mankind was given authority and dominion over all the works of God's hands.

And God blessed them, and God said unto them, Be fruitful, and multiply, and replenish the earth, and subdue it: and have dominion over the fish of the sea, and over the fowl of the air, and over every living thing that moveth upon the earth. (Genesis 1:28)

Authority comes with responsibility. Though man was at the pinnacle of creation, he had to submit to God's command.

And the Lord God commanded the man, saying, Of every tree of the garden thou mayest freely eat: But of the tree of the knowledge of good and evil, thou shalt not eat of it: for in the day that thou eatest thereof thou shalt surely die. (Genesis 2:16-17)

In our first section, we have discussed

that Adam could not eat from the Tree of Knowledge. However, the serpent deceived his wife.

Subsequently, he ate the tree also. God's command was broken, and sin entered into the world.

> *Wherefore, as by one man sin entered into the world, and death by sin; and so death passed upon all men, for that all have sinned. (Romans 5:12)*

Again, once sin entered into the world, man became increasingly wicked. Their thoughts and imaginations brought forth evil. Thus, God decided to remove man from the earth.

And God saw that the wickedness of man was great in the earth, and that every imagination of the thoughts of his heart was only evil continually. And it repented the Lord that he had made man on the earth, and it grieved him at his heart. And the Lord said, I will destroy man whom I have created from the face of the earth; both man, and beast, and the creeping thing, and the fowls of the air; for it repenteth me that I have made them. (Genesis 6:5-7)

In His anger, God sends a flood upon the whole earth. He kills every living creature upon the earth except Noah, his family, and the animals with him in the ark.

The Presentation of the Covenant

After the Flood and the receding of the waters, Noah and all with him in the ark walked upon dry land.

And God spake unto Noah, saying, Go forth of the ark, thou, and thy wife, and thy sons , and thy sons' wives with thee. Bring forth with thee every living thing that is with thee, of all flesh, both of fowl, and of cattle, and of every creeping thing that creepeth upon the earth; that they may breed abundantly in the earth, and be fruitful, and multiply upon the earth. (Genesis 8:15-17)

After these things, we read of Noah's sacrifice to the Lord.

And Noah builded an altar unto the Lord; and took of every clean beast, and of every clean fowl, and offered burnt offerings on the altar. (Genesis 8:20)

The Prelude to the Covenant

In his gratitude for God's salvation, Noah makes a sacrifice. Noah's sacrifice sets the stage for the covenant that God would establish. After the sacrifice, God sets new standards for creation, these included:

1) *The earth would not be cursed because of man.*

The Flood destroyed the contents of the earth. God promises that the earth would not have to pay for man's sins. This sentiment is echoed in the Book of Revelation. The angles were commanded not to hurt the earth as they executed God's judgment.

> *And it was commanded them that they should not hurt the grass of the earth, neither any green thing, neither any tree; but only those men which have not the seal of God in their foreheads. (Revelation 9:4)*

2) *God would not destroy every living creature again.*

Not only did the earth receive a promise, but the living creatures upon it.

They would not be punished, likewise, for the sins of man. Not every kind of living creature would suffer again in the same manner.

> ...*neither will I again smite any more everything living, as I have done. (Genesis 8:21a)*

3) *The seasons would remain as long as the earth.*

To establish the first two promises, God states that the seasons will continue. As long as the earth spins on its axis, the seasons will remain.

The Flood interrupted the natural

successions of the seasons since it lasted for approximately five months (from the Flood's start to the water's recession).

> *While the earth remaineth, seedtime and harvest, and cold and heat, and summer and winter and day and night shall not cease. (Genesis 8:22)*

4) *The fear of man would be upon the animals.*

This statement of the Lord a new dimension to His initial commandment to man (Genesis 1:28). At the beginning, He states that man was to have dominion.

Now, He focuses on the animal's perspective of humans. From now on, the animals would walk in fear of humans.

And the fear of you and the dread of you shall be upon every beast of the earth, and upon every fowl of the air, upon all that moveth upon the earth, and upon all the fishes of the sea; into your hand are they delivered. (Genesis 9:2)

5) Animals were now a part of man's diet.

In the beginning, man and beast ate the products of the earth. They only ate herbs of the field and fruit of the trees. Now, man was informed that he could now eat the animals on the earth.

> *Every moving thing that liveth shall be meat for you; even as the green herb have I given you all things. (Genesis 9:3)*

6) *Man was not to eat blood because it represented life.*

God wanted man to respect life. Since life was in the blood, he was to not ingest blood or shed another man's blood.

> *But flesh with the life thereof, which*

is the blood thereof, shall ye not eat. (Genesis 9:4)

7) *Anyone who killed a man would be killed.*

God instituted the first 'judicial' law. Anyone who killed a man was to be executed in return. It is our belief that this was instituted to repeal the ideal that it was permissible to take life without fear of retribution.

And the Lord said unto him, Therefore whosoever slayeth Cain, vengeance shall be taken on him sevenfold. And the Lord set a mark

> upon Cain, lest any finding him should kill him. (Genesis 4:15)

God showed mercy to Cain and marked him so no one would kill him. However, his descendants perceived this to be a catalyst to murder without regard.

> And Lamech said unto his wives, Adah and Zillah, Hear my voice; ye wives of Lamech, hearken unto my speech: for I have slain a man to my wounding, and a young man to my hurt. If Cain shall be avenged sevenfold, truly Lamech seventy and sevenfold. (Genesis 4:23-24)

Lamech, Cain's descendant, cites the mercy shown to Cain to justify his murder. To repeal this mindset, the Lord clearly states the penalty for murder. This introduces us to a biblical truth.

God's law and/or command is notto be violated because He shows mercyto another individual for a similar or same offense.

Though He requires obedience from all, His grace is not to be taken for granted as an excuse to sin.

For he saith to Moses, I will have mercy on whom I will have mercy, and I will have compassion on whom I will have compassion. (Romans 9:15)

What shall we say then? Shall we continue in sin, that grace may abound? (Romans 6:1)

8) Man was to be fruitful and multiply.

In accordance with his first charge to Adam, Noah and his descendants were to repopulate the earth. Though God destroyed the rest of man and the animals, He now wants the earth to be replenished with life.

And God blessed Noah and his sons,

and said unto them, Be fruitful, and multiply, and replenish the earth. (Genesis 9:1)

The Institution of the Covenant

After giving Noah these instructions and directives, God then institutes a covenant to establish His words. This is referred to as the **Noahic Covenant**. This covenant proved to be important to all creation.

And God spake unto Noah, and to his sons with him, saying, And I, behold, I establish my covenant with you, and with your seed after you;

And with every living creature that is with you, of the fowl, of the cattle, and of every beast of the earth with you; from all that go out of the ark, to every beast of the earth. And I will establish my covenant with you, neither shall all flesh be cut off any more by the waters of a flood; neither shall there any more be a flood to destroy the earth. (Genesis 9:8-11)

Notes:

-Lesson 2-
For in these Things, I Delight

The Covenants Speak

God came into covenant with man and all of creation. This covenant can also be referred to as God's ***covenant of peace*** with all of creation. The question remains, "Why did God establish this covenant?" He had no obligation to do so. He established it because of His character. God does not have to answer to anyone for His actions.

Who hath directed the spirit of the Lord, or being his counselor hath taught him? With whom took he counsel, and who instructed him, and taught him in the path of judgment, and taught him knowledge, and shewed to him the way of understanding? (Isaiah 40:13-14)

In addition, Noah and his sons did not ask God for a guarantee or promise. He did it because of His righteous character.

But let him who glories glory in this, that he understands and knows Me (personally and practically, directly discerning and recognizing My character), that I am the Lord who practices loving-kindness, judgment, and righteousness in the earth; for in these things I delight, says the Lord. *(Jeremiah 9:24 Amplified)*

God's institution of this covenant helps to understand the nature of God. Though there are many attributes to the character of God, three best describe Him. They are holiness, righteousness, and love. These attributes of God provide an answer to the proposed question.

Holiness Causes the Covenant

One of the greatest designations of God is that He is holy. The holiness of God describes the purity in His actions and works. Because He is holy, His creation is to reflect His holiness.

> *Speak unto all the congregation of the children of Israel, and say unto them, Ye shall be holy: for I the Lord your God am holy. (Leviticus 19:2)*

Thus, when God instituted this covenant, He was exemplifying His holiness unto man and creation. Though He destroyed the population of man and beast from the earth, there was no wickedness in Him. He could establish this covenant as a sign of His holy actions upon the unholy populace of earth.

Righteousness Causes the Covenant

God instituted this covenant because of His righteousness. The righteousness of God describes His purity in judgment.

> *But the Lord of hosts shall be exalted in judgment, and God that is holy shall be sanctified in righteousness. (Isaiah 5:16)*

His judgment of man's acts was just. It was not without cause or provocation. His installment of the covenant came to establish that He had acted in righteousness and would continue to do so.

Love Causes the Covenant

The third attribute of God's character fully develops the reason for the establishment of the Noahic Covenant. God is not only governed by love, but He *is* love.

> *Beloved, let us love one another: for love is of God; and every one that loveth is born of God, and knoweth God. He that loveth not knoweth not God; for God is love. (1 John 4:7-8)*

God established this covenant with

man and beast to declare His love for all of His creation. This covenant shows the borderless love that comes from God. Though He was angry, it could not overpower the love that He had for all the works of His hands. Because of His righteousness, holiness, and love, God instituted the Noahic Covenant as a sign of peace between Him and His creation.

The Covenants Speak

Notes:

The Covenants Speak

-Lesson 3-

But Noah Found Grace

When God established the different covenants, He would choose an individual to receive and reveal the covenant to others. The main character of the Noahic Covenant, of course, is **Noah**. However, we discover that when God spoke the constitution (content) of the covenant, it was also to his sons who were with him.

(And God spake unto Noah, and to his sons - Genesis 9:8a).

Noah's Example before the Covenant

Noah was the first son of Lamech, the son of Methuselah (Genesis 5:28-29). At his birth, his father named him according to a prophetic word that would prove true in his life. Lamech prophesied that Noah would comfort man concerning his labors. Man's labor was hard because of the curse laid upon him.

> *And Lamech lived an hundred eighty and two years, and begat a son: And he called his name Noah, saying, This same shall comfort us concerning our work and toil of our hands, because of the ground which the Lord hath cursed. (Genesis 5:28-29)*
>
> *And unto Adam he said, Because thou hast hearkened unto the voice*

of thy wife, and hast eaten of the tree, of which I commanded thee, saying, Thou shalt not eat of it: cursed is the ground for thy sake... (Genesis 3:17a)

Lamech's prophecy was fulfilled in Noah when God spoke to him after the Flood. Noah's sacrificed moved the Lord to revoke the curse of the ground. This would inevitably make man's labors easier.

And the Lord smelled a sweet savor; and the Lord said in his heart, I will not again curse the ground any more for man's sake. (Genesis 8:21)

Noah was a righteous man. The New Testament refers to him as a preacher of righteousness.

And spared not the old world, but saved Noah the eighth person, a preacher of righteousness, bringing in the flood upon the world of the ungodly. (II Peter 2:5)

When God determined to bring the Flood, it is recorded that he found grace in God's sight. This is a clear sign of Noah's righteousness. Noah had three attributes that reflected that he was a servant of the Lord: *faith, obedience, and worship*. Noah was a man of faith in relationship with the Lord. God spoke to him through their established relationship.

> *By faith Noah, being warned of God of things not seen as yet, moved with fear, prepared an ark to the saving of his house; by the which he condemned the world, and became heir of the righteousness which is by faith. (Hebrews 11:7)*

God considered Noah out of all the men on the face of the earth. Thus,

Noah's faith and walk with the Lord is evidenced again in that God's favor was upon him.

> *But Noah found grace in the eyes of the Lord. These are the generations of Noah: Noah was a just man and perfect in his generations, and Noah walked with God. (Genesis 6:8-9)*

Noah is called just and perfect. He acted in righteousness and was just in his interactions with others. Noah was just in light of the continual wickedness around him. Noah walked in obedience as a sign of his faith.

When God told him of the coming destruction, Noah responded in obedience. He built the ark in spite of any criticisms and questions. He did it in light of the fact that he had not ever seen rain. He believed the Lord in spite of his personal experience.

And every plant of the field before it was in the earth, andevery herb of the field before it grew: for the Lord God had not caused it to rain upon the earth, and there was not a man to till the ground. But there went up a mist from the earth and watered the whole face of the ground. (Genesis 2:5-6)

Until this time, no man had ever seen rain. The earth was watered by a mist. However, he obeyed the Lord.

And God said unto Noah, The end of all flesh is come before me; for the earth is filled with violence through them; and, behold, I will destroy them with the earth. Make thee an ark of gopher wood; rooms shalt thou make in the ark, and shalt pitch it within and without with pitch. (Genesis 6:13-14)

For 120 years, Noah built the ark and warned men of the coming destruction. After the Flood, Noah worshipped through his sacrifice.

And Noah builded an altar unto the Lord; and took of every clean beast, and of every clean fowl, and offered burnt offerings on the altar. (Genesis 8: 20)

Noah's Example after the Covenant

Noah demonstrated his respect and reverence for the Lord in his obedience and sacrifice. His life serves as an example to the Christian. Jesus taught concerning the last days by referring to Noah.

> *But as the days of Noe were, so shall also the coming of the Son of man be. For as in the days that were before the flood they were eating and drinking, marrying and giving in marriage, until the day that Noe entered into the ark, And knew not until the flood came, and took them all away; so shall also the coming of the Son of man be. (Matthew 24:37-39)*

The Covenants Speak

The Example of Noah	The Example of New Testament Believer
Noah found grace in the sight of the ord. (Genesis 6:8)	Through faith, believers are saved by the grace of God. We now stand in His grace. (Eph. 2:8)
Noah was a just and perfect man. (Genesis 6:9)	The Christian is to walk in holiness and righteousness. They are to reflect the perfect nature of God. (Matthew. 5:48)
Noah was warned of God's judgment. (Genesis 6:13)	The Christian is warned of Christ's Return and God's judgment of all man. (II Peter 3:1-13)
Noah was instructed to build an ark for salvation (Gen 6:1	The Christian 'builds an ark' through faith and obedience to Christ. (I John 3:1-3)

Noah was a preacher of righteousness. He warned men for their salvation. (II Peter 2:5)	The Christian has to be a witness for Christ and the gospel. (Matthew. 28:19-20)
Noah sacrificed unto the Lord. (Genesis 8:20)	The Christian offers up spiritual sacrifices (praise, giving, and good works) unto God through Jesus. (I Peter 2:5)

He said that it would be as it was in the days of Noah. Thus, if Noah found grace and escaped the Flood, the believer should follow his example to overcome. On the previous page, we have included a diagram outlining how Noah's life reflects the Christian's relationship to Christ under the New Covenant.

Noah reflects the character of the New Testament believer and gives us a foreshadowing of the 2nd Advent of Jesus Christ.

Notes:

The Covenants Speak

-Lesson 4-

This Is the Token of the Covenant

Since covenants are similar to contractual agreements, they have conditions and terms. The Noahic Covenant does not differ. To understand God's intent for this covenant, an examination of its constitution is necessary. The Noahic Covenant contains two main components.

The Promises of the Covenant

The first part of the covenant included a promise to man, beast, and the earth. God promised that the waters of a flood would not destroy creation.

And I will establish my covenant

with you, neither shall all flesh be cut off any more by the waters of a flood; neither shall there any more be a flood to destroy the earth. (Genesis 9:11)

Why did God make such a promise? To man, rain was a sign of God's judgment. Since rain would continue to fall on the earth, God assured man that he did not have to fear for his life when he saw it.

Noah and his family were not to fear rain again. In addition, when they told their descendants the story, they would not fear that it would happen again.

Unlike the other covenants, this is the only covenant that involved a promise to all of creation, namely the living creatures of the earth. God included all of creation in this covenant. The creatures would experience this covenant of peace. They, too, had a part in God's purpose in the earth.

And God spake unto Noah, and to his sons with him, saying, And I, behold, I establish my covenant with you, and with your seed after you; And with every living creature that is with you, of the fowl, of the cattle, and of every beast of the earth with you; from all that go out of the ark, to every beast of the earth. (Genesis 9:8-10)

God expressed His love for all of His creation. The living creatures could experience God's assurance in this covenant. This leads us to some great truths concerning God and creation.

Just as God uses humans in His eternal purpose, the same applies to animals. When God wanted to sustain Elijah in th e time of famine, He used the ravens.

> *And it shall be, that thou shalt drink of the brook; and I have commanded the ravens to feed thee there. And the ravens brought him bread and flesh in the morning, and bread and flesh in the evening; and he drank of the brook. (I Kings 17:4, 6)*

When God wanted to stop Balaam from going to curse Israel, He allowed his donkey to see the angel and speak to him. The donkey knew what the angel of the Lord had come to do.

And the ass saw the angel of the Lord standing in the way, and his sword drawn in his hand: and the ass turned aside out of the way, and went into the field: and Balaam smote the ass, to turn her into the way. (Numbers 22:23)

But was rebuked for his iniquity: the dumb ass speaking with man's voice forbad the madness of the prophet. (II Peter 2:16)

When God revealed to Daniel the things that were to come, He used images of animals and living creatures to reflect the coming kingdoms and their rulers.

Daniel spake and said, I saw in my vision by night, and, behold, the four winds of the heaven strove upon the great sea. And four great beasts came up from the sea, diverse one from another. (Daniel 7:2-3)

To execute His judgment upon disobedient prophets, He used lions.

And when the prophet that brought him back from the way heard thereof, he said, It is the man of

God, who was disobedient unto the word of the Lord: therefore the Lord hath delivered him unto the lion, which hath torn him, and slain him, according to the word of the Lord, which he spake unto him. (I Kings 13:26)

And a certain man of the sons of the prophets said unto his neighbour in the word of the Lord, Smite me, I pray thee. And the man refused to smite him. Then said he unto him, Because thou hast not obeyed the voice of the Lord, behold, as soon as thou art departed from me, a lion shall slay thee. And as soon as he was departed from him, a lion found him, and slew him. (I Kings 20:35-36)

Jesus' birth was punctuated with the presence of animals. Man made no room for Him, but creatures did. He was born in a place where animals resided and placed in a manger, which was is a trough from which livestock ate. This also foreshadows creation's place in God's redemptive plan.

And she brought forth her firstborn son, and wrapped him in swaddling clothes, and laid him in a manger; because there was no room for them in the inn. (Luke 2:7)

His triumphal entrance into Jerusalem would not take place except He came in on a donkey. When He sent the disciples to retrieve the animal, Jesus expressed His need for the animal. The animal was needed to fulfill prophecy; that is, God's eternal purpose.

And when they drew nigh unto Jerusalem, and were come to Bethphage, unto the mount of Olives, then sent Jesus two disciples,

Saying unto them, Go into the village over against you, and straightway ye shall find an ass tied, and a colt with her: loose them, and bring them unto me. And if any man say ought unto you, ye shall say, The Lord hath need of them; and straightway he will send them. All this was done, that it might be fulfilled which was spoken by the prophet, saying, Tell ye the daughter of Sion, Behold, thy King cometh unto thee, meek, and sitting upon an ass, and a colt the foal of an ass. (Matthew 21:1-5)

God uses creation to fulfill His purposes. In addition, we find that creation, along with believers, is awaiting the coming of the Lord.

For the earnest expectation of the creature waiteth for the manifestation of the sons of God. For the creature was made subject to vanity, not willingly, but by reason of him who hath subjected the same in hope, Because the creature itself also shall be delivered from the bondage of corruption into the glorious liberty of the children of God. For we know that the whole creation groaneth and travaileth in pain together until now. (Romans 8:19-22)

Since creation was put into bondage because of man's sin. It now expects to be liberated. Even in the end, creation shall be liberated along with the children of God.

Because of these things, we understand why God's covenant and promise involved all of creation. The second part of the covenant's constitution involves the token or sign of the covenant.

The Sign of the Covenant

God outlines the terms of the covenant with Noah and his sons. To demonstrate that the covenant would not be violated, God said that a token or sign would be given.

> *And God said, This is the token of the covenant which I make between me and you and every living creature that is with you, for perpetual generations: I do set my bow in the cloud, and it shall be for a token of a covenant between me and the earth. (Genesis 9:12-13)*

God states that He would place His bow in the cloud. Today, we refer to it as the rainbow because it appears most frequently after the rain. God's use of a bow is not at random. It is reflective of God laying down His bow of war against man until the final Day of Judgment.

To ensure that man would not be fearful of judgment when they saw the rain, God said He would cause His bow to been seen in the clouds when it rained.

Scientists today refute the biblical account of the rainbow because it can be explained through scientific observation and analysis. In school, we are taught how the rainbow appears.

The rainbow's appearance is caused by dispersion of sunlight as raindrops refract it. The different refractions of light appear then as color. The rainbow is readily observed when the viewer is at a lower altitude. Scientists refer to the refractions appearing in colors as an optical phenomenon.

This means it can only be explained with a certain level of clarity. We want to make a declaration to all who choose scientific observation over biblical revelation

Because science/scientists can explain it does not mean that God is not the author of it!

And it shall come to pass, when I bring a cloud over the earth, that the bow shall be seen in the cloud: And I will remember my covenant, which is between me and you and every living creature of all flesh; and the waters shall no more become a flood to destroy all flesh. (Genesis 9:14-15)

Even though other events can

produce the rainbow effect (appearance of a rainbow), rainbows are most frequently seen when it rains and there is a cloud formation. This establishes the words of the Lord. The sign of the covenant represents peace between God and His creation. God will not execute final judgment until Christ's return.

Notes:

The Covenants Speak

-Lesson 5-

The Covenant and the Faith

The Noahic Covenant has not ended. The conclusion of this covenant will not be until the end of this age. Unlike some of the other covenants in scripture, the Noahic Covenant does not involve a response from man. God initiated this covenant and established it with the sign of the rainbow.

This covenant was made with all non-believers with all creatures are partakers of this covenant. Noah and his experiences, including the institution of the Noahic Covenant help us to understand parts of Christianity.

To conclude the examination, we will explore two aspects of this truth.

Noah's Example Reflects the Christian Faith

1) The Flood, which cleansed the earth, represents the Ordinance of Baptism that demonstrates our faith repentance and faith before God.

> *Which sometime were disobedient, when once the longsuffering of God waited in the days of Noah, while the ark was a preparing, wherein few, that is, eight souls were saved by water. The like figure whereunto*

> *even baptism doth also now save us (not the putting away of the filth of the flesh, but the answer of a good conscience toward God,) by the resurrection of Jesus Christ. (I Peter 3:20-21)*

2) Noah's faith is an example to believers who must endure in this present age.

> *By faith Noah, being warned of God of things not seen as yet, moved with fear, prepared an ark to the saving of his house; by the which he condemned the world, and became*

heir of the righteousness which is by faith. (Hebrews 11:7)

Noah's Experience Reflects the End Times and Judgment

1) If God judged the earth before, He will do it again at the end of this age. Noah escaped the judgment of that time. Christians will escape God's final judgment.

> *And spared not the old world, but saved Noah the eighth person, a preacher of righteousness, bringing in the flood upon the world of the ungodly. (II Peter 2:5)*

2) Jesus said before His coming, the world would be as it was in Noah's Day.

> *But as the days of Noah were, so shall also the coming of the Son of man be. For as in the days that were before the flood they were eating and drinking, marrying and giving in marriage, until the day that Noah entered into the ark, And knew not until the flood came, and took them all away; so shall also the coming of the Son of man be. (Matthew 24:37-39)*

Noah's life, example, and the covenant bearing his name provide vital illumination for Christians today.

The Noahic Covenant demonstrates God's love and intention of peace between Him and His creation. The earth and all of its inhabitants are partakers of it until this present day.

Notes:

The Covenants Speak

Bibliography

Merriam-Webster Online Dictionary. Copyright © 2005 by Merriam-Webster, Incorporated. All rights reserved.

The Bible Library. Copyright 1988 – 2000.Ellis Enterprises Incorporated, 4205 McAuley Blvd., Suite 385, Oklahoma City, OK 73120, (405) 749-0273. All Rights Reserved.

Lockman Foundation. *Comparative Study Bible.* Zondervan Publishing House.

Grand Rapids, MI, c1984

Smith, William. *Smith's Bible Dictionary.* Holman Bible Publishers. Nashville, TN. c1994

Notes:

The Covenants Speak

www.ingramcontent.com/pod-product-compliance
Lightning Source LLC
Chambersburg PA
CBHW050341010526
44119CB00049B/646